Eight Mistakes Women Make in Relationships

A Woman's Guide to Getting it Right

Tony A Gaskins Sr.

Eight Mistakes Women Make in Relationships

Copyright © 2011 by Tony A Gaskins Sr.

ISBN 978-0-9844822-3-8

Dedicated to:
Princess Amiah Gaskins
Taliyah Amare Gaskins
Tony A. Gaskins III

Foreword

I remember growing up with my Father in the home and having to sit and listen to him talk for hours on end. He is so full of wisdom that he can literally talk you through a night. Whenever I needed to know something or he had to teach me a lesson on life he would pour into my spirit from his. He talked with me so much that it wasn't long before I started to think like him. Everything I did I would ask myself before I did it, what would my daddy do. I look up to him and respect him with the utmost respect. I am proud to carry his name. He is such a good Father that I wish I could clone him and spread him throughout the world. I remember growing up and wishing that I could share him with every other young boy around who didn't have a Father like him. I remember taking the lessons I learned from him and teaching them to my friends who didn't have a Father in the home and they would sit and listen as if they were receiving a word from God. I remember growing up and listening to other ministers and teachers and thinking to myself, wow none of these men have the wisdom that my Father has but yet the people don't know his name. I always hoped that he would sit down and take a little time out for himself and put his wisdom on paper and I'm so glad that he finally did. He is more of a talker than a typer and I know there were some great things lost in transmission while going from his mind to these pages so I hope that his next step will be to speak around the world and touch the lives of millions just as he has touched mine. I'm still growing and learning and trying to wrap my mind around the things that he tries to teach me, but I hope that one day I will get there. He gives me so much praise for my work and the things that I'm doing but I don't think he knows that I honor and admire him more than words can express. I can hardly see what I'm typing because the tears of joy and admiration that fills my eyes. I'm glad to finally be able to share my Father with the world and I hope that you can walk away from this book with some insight that you didn't have before you picked it up. I'm hoping that there will be many more books to come and that each time he will get a little more comfortable with this form of teaching and be able to leave all of him on the pages to be read by people long after he is gone. I'm proud that my Father will go down in history and that somewhere his book will always be. I introduce to you my loving Father, Tony A. Gaskins Sr.

Table of Contents

Introduction

T here are eight problem areas that I have discovered concerning women as they pertain to
relationships. I have also found that women engage in
these problem areas inadequately informed and with
misconceived experiences. I will share a wealth of
knowledge and experiences that I have learned, gained
and studied over the past thirty-three years. I have
chosen to do so because of my love for God and my
God-given respect and admiration for women. These
two things have driven my desire to balance the
relationship playing field by informing women of
things they should know from a perspective different
than their own. There are eight areas in a woman's life
concerning relationships where she continues to error.
Not knowing *"what you are"* is where we will begin
because most women do not even realize what they
are, nor the devastating effects that not knowing can
have on their lives. Then we will look at the remaining

1

chapters: *"What he is," "Who I am," Redefine and recreate," "Increasing my values," "Increasing my worth," "Protecting my worth,"* and finally, *"Connecting my worth."* All of these mistakes may presently apply to you, or perhaps some of them do and some of them don't right now. Think of this is like a buffet; use what applies, and read the rest now to use for later. It is better to know and not need, than to need and not know.

Although each one of these is important, they all have different relationship significance. For example, some have *foundational significance*, which are building blocks for relationships, things that a relationship must contain in order for it to be a relationship. Others have *informational significance*, information you can add to your relationship to customize it to thrive in the best way it can.

Thank you very much for all your hard work,
Tony Gaskins

The Eight Mistakes

1. Not knowing what you are
2. Not knowing what a man is
3. Not knowing who you are
4. Failing to redefine you and recreate yourself
5. Failing to increase your values
6. Failing to increase your worth
7. Failing to protect your worth
8. Failing to properly connect your worth

1. Not knowing what you are

We will first work on you as the person, and then you as the woman. You as the person are *what you are*, and you as the woman are *who you are*. Knowing "who you are" is largely based on learned behaviors and nurturing, while "what you are" is largely based on nature or creative genetics. Knowing who you are allows you to understand your determined wants and desires. Knowing what you are allows you to understand what has already been determined for you by nature. Although it is important to know who you are (because not knowing who you are can get you into the wrong relationship with the wrong person), not knowing what you are is what causes you to do all the wrong things that you do while you are in those relationships. So we will first address the "what," and then the "who," because the "what" is also the "why." *What* you are is *why* you do some of the things you do in relationships. Women share many commonalities concerning relationships that may have been misconceived to be individualities. Concepts such as loving hard, falling fast and deeply in love, trying too hard to make it work, staying in the wrong relationships for the wrong reasons, staying in relationships too long, ignoring red flags, repeatedly reengaging in relationships with the same guy who has already proven to be a failure are all part of an endless list. All of these behaviors are by-products of what you are. So what are you? Well, first let me say this: I believe in my heart that the woman is one of God's greatest creations, if not the greatest.

People often wonder why God only used one of Adam's ribs to create the woman. Could a whole woman really be comprised of such a small portion of the man? Obviously not; it stands to reason that if He only used a little bit of the man, He had to use a great deal of something else. After all, He wasn't making another man, so the less he used of the man, the less she would be like the man. In fact, they are almost totally different. God, who knows all things and has the master plan, knew exactly what He was creating. He knew He was making something different, something special, something unique and something very important.

He was not just making another life; He was constructing a perpetual gift of life, to life, and for life. It was a gift to man and for mankind, in my personal, professional and theological opinion. The woman is God's greatest and most significant miracle which continues to perform today. Why? Because she is the vessel He has chosen to bring life into this world; without her, there would be no life. There would be no Presidents of the United States of America, nor any other government leaders, pastors or teachers. That, in itself, is an indication of the importance and necessity of her existence. However, in order for her to fulfill her designed purpose, there must be a man in her life. There has to be a relationship, hopefully followed by marriage, copulation, and then the miracle of reproduction. But there is a problem.

In today's society, more and more women are choosing to refrain from relationships. Their decision however, is based on more of a forced choice, rather than a first choice. It is usually after several failed relationship attempts when this decision is reached. Truth be known, it's really not relationships that they don't want, it's the relation-trips, the hurt, pain and drama associated with the relationships. However, their efforts to refrain from relationships, no matter how diligent or sincere, are usually futile. Why? Because a woman's nature (not just her body) was created to have sex. To phrase it more euphemistically, it was created to bear children. Why? To populate the world. Why? Because otherwise, we would not exist. Pardon my candor and encapsulated analogy, but it is important to get right to the point in order to focus on the problem and reach the solution. The fundamental point is that our bodies are designed to want sex. The dilemma is that when a woman makes that physical connection, she inevitably also makes an emotional connection usually far beyond the emotional connection of her male counterpart. This typically leads to an undesired and oppositional demised relationship. Many women believe that the solution is to plan not to get in another relationship. At this point, your body can enable its psychological defense mechanism known as sublimation, which is designed to help you deal with reality crises. This will allow you to redirect those sexual impulses through some other exertion, such as working more or enjoying a hobby. Believe it or not, that will not last forever, and will eventually prove to be beyond your control. Your body, mind and emotions will eventually desire to be in a relationship. The solution is for you to find a compatible man in order to have a successful relationship.

Women, in general, enter relationships with pure and honest expectations only later to become victims of the travesty of the failed relationship suffered from entering into them with ill-intentioned men who enter into relationships with a predetermined level of commitment. Even though women in general are born relationship material, men are not, thus creating a need for women to protect themselves from these types of experiences by arming themselves with the knowledge of the behavior and actions of these men. So why do women do what they do in relationships? Why do they love so hard, make sincere commitments, and go above and beyond the call of duty to make their relationships work? Because that's what a woman is. She is a connector. The nature of a woman is to make connections, commitments, attachments and adjustments. God has innately given her these attributes to accommodate her created ability to bear and care for her children. After all, he has appointed her to be the gateway of life. Her body naturally commences to prepare for, provide for, and to protect the offspring. That life comes into this world in the form of a helpless and totally dependant infant. And even though she is not the only bearer when it concerns offspring, God has given her the nature to nurture the longest, in excess of twenty years. Because of the woman's creative design, she literally makes a physical connection with her child. This connection is via an umbilical cord, and although this cord will be severed, it is superseded by two much greater connections, one being emotional, the other spiritual. The emotional connection is a mentally aware demonstrational response to sensory impulses of passion which attach, develops and performs acts of love and kindness. She is also connected spiritually by an unconditional binding love and commitment. This is not just what she does, this is what she is. This is also why she loves the way she loves, and does the things she does in her relationships. It explains why she commits the way she does, connects the way she does, attaches the way she does, loves so hard and so real. It is due to how she is created, and unless something drastically happens to alter that, it is how she will continue to love.

Although God created us with a desire for sex, it was meant to be done according to His divine plan within healthy, successful, compatible marriages (see my book *Unequally Yoked*). However, the intrinsic and perpetual drive for sex and relationship are not contingent upon religion or salvation. It is given without bias to all of mankind. Having said that, let's revisit our three aspects of discussion: the point, the problem, and the solution. The point is that sex is the catalyst for relationship. It may not always be the catalyst for the woman, but I can assure you that it is usually the catalyst for the man.

So, even though relationships/marriages are God's institution, there is a problem, a rather large problem; monogamous perpetual relationships. More and more, women are choosing not to be in relationships because of the problems associated with them. God meant for your relationship to last until one of you dies from natural causes. Coincidentally, most women would want that to be the case also. However, the average woman by age 40 has experienced an average of five failed relationships. Now, of course the numbers may not be the same for the men, but even if the numbers were virtually similar, the effects would not be the same because men and women, in general and by nature, do not approach relationships in the same way. A relationship is meant to be the same for the man and the woman, but it is perceived differently by both of them. Because of this, the failed relationship usually has a much more devastating effect on the woman rather than the man. A failed relationship can affect a woman psychologically, emotionally, physically, financially and even career-wise. In other words, it can affect all of her, while having very little effect on the man. So therefore, when concerning relationships, women have to be really careful, because they do not possess the same psychological or emotional systems as their male Homo sapiens counterparts. They have a much more sensitive, sincere and binding emotional system. They have a much greater desire for commitment, and a greater ability for monogamous relationships than the man. Why does she hurt the most? There's a scripture that says, "Where much is given, much is required." Regarding relationships, women usually give the most 99% of the time.

If I were to choose one word that describes a woman, I would say "connector." Women literally make connections. This is important to know because after experiencing several failed relationship, women often wonder if something is wrong with them, what they could have done differently, or they blame themselves for not doing or being enough. In actuality, the problem lies with the man the majority of the time. As for the woman in the relationship, she loves more, commits more, gives more, wants more and expects more. William Shakespeare said, "Some are born great, some become great, and some have greatness thrust upon them." It is quite obvious that William Shakespeare's topic was greatness, but this is true with anything. In this case, women are born having much more necessary essentials for successful relationships, making them relationship material. On the contrary, men have to *become* relationship material. Although men have the drive and desire to be in relationships, they lack the interest to pursue the qualities and other essentials needed to be positive, determining, productive parts of the relationship. So men have to work hard (some harder than others), and more often than not, they fail to apply the necessary effort until it is too late or the relationship is already in a state of crisis. Frequently, men just don't get it, and have to be taught the qualities and essentials needed for healthy relationships.

While a woman does have much more inherent relationship essentials, she does lack in two very crucial areas: 1) Not knowing the mind of the man when it concerns love and 2) Not knowing her heart when it concerns love. This combination equals hurt, pain and disappointment in relationships. Getting to know your heart regarding relationships is getting to know you. While it is important to know who you are, it is more important to know *what* you are.

Who you are has to do more with your nurturing rather than your nature. Your nurturing is more about learned behaviors, while your nature has more to do with your genetics, source traits, and surface traits. What you are is not about your learned behaviors, source or surface traits, but rather about your created make-up. Knowing what you are is essential to knowing what you do. You know you are a woman, and you know he is a man. You know that there is a difference, but what is the difference? Knowing what the difference is holds much more importance than knowing there is a difference.

If someone showed you a picture of you and a fish and asked you to identify yourself, you would be able to do that without a problem. You know who you are.

If they asked you if there is a difference, you would be able to tell them the difference. You're a person, and it's a fish. If they asked you what the difference is, you would not be able to give them a definitive answer unless you were informed about fishes, what they are, and what you are.

However, by knowing about the fish, you would know that you two could not be in a relationship, due to incompatibility. You would know that the fish needs water to live, and you need air, that your appetites are different, communications are different, and even mating practices are different. Even though you have lots more obvious things in common with your Homo sapiens counterpart, such as the fact that you both breathe air, share the same type of environment, eat the same food sources, and mate in the same type of way, there are still enough differences to keep a relationship from working. What are the differences? This is much easier to answer if you know what you are and what he is. God, in His infinite wisdom, made the man the way He wanted him to be, barring his infidelity (see the next chapter titled, "What he is.") Then He made the woman the way he wanted her to be. Even though they have some similarities, God gave them a host of differences. He gave them different dominating natures, the man of a more outward or external nature and the woman of a more inward or internal nature, as in close and near.

According to God, the bone (rib) of the man was a perpetual bond between the man and the woman, a primal desire and affection, a link of attraction, and a piece of love that he placed in the woman for the man, and of the man for the woman. This love was to be a perpetual love, a never-ending love, one of endurance, longevity and assurance. But there existed then and still is now, an opponent of love, an enemy of love, a deceiver of love, a manipulator of love. This opponent of their love is actually the indifference of the natures.

Who they are is determined by what they are, and what they are is indifference of their natures. What their natures are determines what their love is. So because they have indifferent natures, it causes a conflict in their love. We have three primary emotions. Of the three, love is the most sought after, (the other two emotions are anger and fear.) Both the man and the woman are casualties of love; the woman suffers hurt and pain to say the least, and the man experiences delayed regret and loss of the sensual gratification and companionship he lost from the woman. They both suffer the losses in love due to the lack of attention to the details of love. The Word of God says, "My people perish because of a lack of knowledge." Love perishes, relationships perish, houses perish, money perishes; many things perish because of the lack of knowledge. Neither the man nor the woman is born knowing exactly what love is, and most people still have no clue even after they are grown. It is something we must learn.

Love has a definition. It is very important to know what love is and what love isn't. Then you'll know what love does, and what love doesn't. In almost every case when the woman was involved in a relationship which failed, the man involved did not posses nor exhibit the attributes or characteristics of love. **In other words, he was not in love with you, he was infatuated with you.** Now maybe he thought he loved you, and maybe you thought he did too. But as I noted earlier, love has a definition. My goal is to assist you in knowing what love is by teaching you the characteristics of love. So therefore, if a man does not posses nor display those characteristics, then you will know not to waste your time, and keep it moving.

Let's look at the characteristics of love.

1. *It's giving*; not demanding or requiring. This is first and foremost. This is essential because a man's nature is normally opposite of this; he is selfish and controlling by nature. But it is not for you to accept this; he must be taught the change. It is your responsibility to get what you deserve. I am not teaching you to become selfish by exploiting this. Once you do that, you actually become as he is; this is just about both people being able to equally perform the attributes and characteristics of love; it gives of itself.

2. *It's kind*; men have a nature to argue and fuss unnecessarily. But love is kind. It is conducive to comfort and seeks peace. It is tender, helpful, considerate and agreeable.

3. *It's bearable*; it allows for a person to be themselves, but the best person they can be. This does not mean if he drinks, does drugs, fusses and cusses excessively, that that's acceptable. If he fits that description, then you should reconsider your options. You should

be working to increase your standards and values. Have him come up to being better, not you going down to worse. A man's nature is to change you and to expect you to accept him as he is.

4. *It believes*; it believes in you as you believe in yourself. A man's nature is to control you rather than believe in you.

5. *It endures;* it bears and supports during difficult or disagreeable times. Men tend to walk away in hard or disagreeable times. You need to know that he will not do that.

6. *It's perpetual;* it does not discontinue without a really good reason. A man may see someone younger or more attractive and leave you.

7. *Rejoices in the truth;* you should be able to talk about pending issues, no matter what they may be. Men tend to want to talk about what they want to talk about and on their own terms, and it usually is not going to be the real issues at hand. Make sure you can have a real conversation with him.

8. *It is selfless;* it places others before itself. This is what mothers do all the time for their children. This is also what she does for her husband and this is what he needs to do for you. It's important to know that he can and will sacrifice for you.

   Let's take a look at what love does not do.

9. *It doesn't behave itself unseeingly;* it does not do or ask you to do anything that is not in good taste. It will not ask you to steal or kill or participate in anything considered unacceptable or contrary to the standards of society

10. *It takes no pleasure in iniquity;* it does not like or take pleasure in doing anything that is wrong. It does not commit unjust acts or deeds, nor try to get you to do them.

11. *Think evil;* it does not think suspicious thoughts or say hurtful or harmful things. It does not make demeaning or demoralizing accusations. It does not wish bad or negative things.

12. *Not easily provoked;* it does not participate in "tic for tac." It does not display or incite

irrational emotional response because of an unfavorable thought or uncertain circumstance.

13. ***Does not envy;*** it does not desire something that belongs to someone else. It does not want your significant other to be like someone else for your approval or satisfaction, nor does it feel unhappy or resentful of wanting someone else's success.

14. ***Does not flaunt itself;*** it is not boastful about one's achievements or possessions. It does not show off or flaunt.

15. ***Is not puffed up;*** it does not exaggerate itself, nor does it flatter in vain in order to impress someone else.

Love really has no limits to a mother; she can love her child even though he may have violently murdered someone else's child. Love has no boundaries; a wife can love and support her husband even through his toughest trials or challenges. Love has no restrictions; parents can love their children unconditionally, even after discovering they are homosexual or addicted to drugs. Love does, however, have choices. The supplier can choose to turn off the supply, and even though it does not happen instantly, it will eventually cease and can later be rechanneled to a more suitable source.

God, who is the creator of love and every other gift and emotion, has declared it. He says it is the most essential gift to life that a person can have, give or receive. He said the following as He compared it to other gifts and deeds: *"If you had the gift and ability to speak every language there is, sing with a heavenly voice, could see into the future, understand all mysteries. If you knew everything there was to know, and had all the faith from God that a man can have, is the richest man in the world, fed and clothed all the poor, and was willing to be killed for the Lord, and yet do not have love, then He says all of the things we just mentioned do not mean anything."*

So love is the key. We may wonder why He did not make it more pure in the man, since it is the crucial ingredient in the relationship. If it is the key ingredient in relationships, then trust and believe that God, in His infinite wisdom, did not make a mistake.

So what are some of the benefits of knowing what you are? Well, one advantage is that it helps you to understand why you love the way you do. You now know that you make connections, become attached and become really emotionally involved. As a woman, you carry this connection package whether you are capable of having children or not. This means that in the event of a failed relationship, which is highly likely because the man lack the emotional levels of commitment that you possess, you are a lot more likely to suffer much more hurt and pain than the man. So, what should you do? Consider what you have to give, which is a lot, and make sure that the person who you are partnering with is contributing the same.

2. Not knowing what he is

T he second mistake that women make when it concerns relationships is, not knowing men. This is not a reference to "getting to know" who he says he is. It is about getting to know what nature says he is. This way, you will know what to expect and will not be caught off guard. Men will always offer to tell you what kind of men they are, and of course, a man's report will be biased. A man's report on his own character is equivalent to a car company reporting on the worth of one of its vehicles. Entertain the thought of an unbiased car magazine giving you a consumers' report on the history of problems notorious for a particular car. The average person would certainly want to know and thoroughly check out the report to be sure that those problems are resolved before purchasing the car. That would be the equivalent of nature's report on what kind of person the man is. The first thing you need to know about a man is that his nature easily allows him to lie and deceive, especially in regards to courting a woman. He will gladly and emphatically tell you what you want and need to hear. That's not who he is; that's what he is. This is why it is so imperative that you get to know the man. Although a man is supposed to be your partner in the relationship, you will find more often than not, that he will end up being your opponent. So, it really behooves you to go into the relationship arena seeing him as an opponent and not a friend, at least not until you really get to know him. Once you know him, then you can love him for who you know him to be. Until then, you need to keep your guards up and emotions down. It's not that he doesn't care; he just cares a whole lot more about himself and his primitive needs and desires, more than he does about you and yours. Most of the time, believe it or not, a relationship to the man is like a game. For him, it is simply about winning, by any means necessary. The person with the most points wins, and points for him translates as sex. For you, points equal him getting to know and respect you and for you to know and respect him. The goal for him is to score the most points, and as quickly as he can. Sex is a touchdown for him, and he wants to win desperately. Now, as with any successful teams in sports, you have to know your opponent. You must know their strengths and weaknesses in order to neutralize or capitalize on them. A successful team has to be able to defend or protect its own goal. Like so, it is your responsibility to protect yourself. To do so, you must know your opponent. To reiterate, one of the most vital things you need to know about relationship, if not the most important, is the man. Because when it concerns the relationship, he ultimately makes or breaks it. It takes two; you can't do it alone.

So let's get to know the man. We will examine the first, second, and third most important things you need to know about the man. First, he is *motivated and driven by sex*. Second, he is *motivated and driven by sex*. And third, he is *motivated and driven by sex*. What you must understand is that this fact is not a problem within itself, because women want and desire sex as well. However, the problem is what he does and will do to get it. He will literally lie, cheat and steal. He will lie while looking you in the eyes. He will cheat on you if he encounters another woman who he wants to sex. And he will steal in the process; steal your heart with his words, efforts and actions. In many cases, when it's all said and done, he may have also stolen your confidence and faith in the relationship.

So the first three things that I am redundantly telling you and want you to understand about the man are that when he accosts you, it is for sex. I am not going to sugarcoat it or water it down. Many women get offended when receiving this information, because they feel that I'm saying that the men with whom they are currently involved or the men who approach them are only interested in them for sex, and see them as sex objects and not for who they really are. Well, that's pretty much the sum of it, and what I am telling you is the truth. If the relationship can last long enough and withstand its conflicts, then he may develop true and loving feelings, but initially, men are all about sex. In many cases, that is what it remains to be about, and that is the hard truth. If someone tells me that there is a state called California, and since I have never visited California, I choose to believe that it does not exist, that does not in any way change the fact that it actually does exist. This does not mean that you are not an outstanding woman with outstanding qualities. It just means that he is not interested in your values, morals or qualities at this time; he's just interested in sex. In due time, you can possibly make him grow interested in those deeper qualities that make up your character as a woman, but initially, he just wants sex.

The man has a different nature than the woman. His nature has a different effect on his behavior than the woman's nature has on her. These are behaviors of nature. The first behavior of nature that you need to be aware of is that *he loves differently than you.* We discussed what real love is in the first chapter. For the man, love, *real* love, is going to be an emotion that he is going to have to learn. His insatiable desire for sex chokes out his normal senses for real love. He knows that what he feels is not real love because he knows it is not fair love. The reason it's not fair is because he is not really concerned about you or how you feel; it's about him. His success comes in being able to make you feel and believe that it is indeed about you. He is able to do this by employing his most effective emotion, *affection.* Affection mirrors and represents itself as real love, but it is not. It's able to be thoughtful, warm, caring and even display regard. But it does not have the qualities of love, such as the enduring sacrifices and commitment that love possesses. Nevertheless, he will represent this affection as love, express it as love, and certainly confess it as love. But rarely does he ever mean it; he says what he says to eventually and ultimately get sex. Sex to him is like food. He may love to dine at this particular restaurant, or perhaps several restaurants, but he's not interested in buying the restaurants, nor learning how to cook for that matter; he is content with just eating the food. When he does love or fall in love, it's conditional. It is based on what he feels is right, what he feels is fair, and what he feels is appropriate. The problem in this is that what he feels is usually biased and in favor of himself.

This brings us to the next behavior of nature; *competitiveness.* He is competitive by nature; it is an innate behavior and emotion. Because of his competitive nature, everything is a competition, and he has to win. He is competing with everyone, including you and himself. When men go on trips or vacations, do you ever notice how in a hurry they are? They drive fast, and they don't want to stop for anything until they have conquered a certain amount of miles in a certain amount of time. He is always competing. The unwritten rule is he that has the most points win. That is why men often don't want to let go even when the relationship is over. That is why they beg, cry, plead and profess to have changed in all the necessary areas. Typically, this is just to get you back, which is actually to keep you from being with someone else. Losing you to someone else would mean that he lost. So in a case such as this, a man will attempt to get the game to a point where it doesn't mean anything to him. Then, it becomes a loss he can live with. That is why men often revert to their old ways once they get you back, because the mission is accomplished. It is not because of anything you've done; they've usually found someone new. That is just part of their nature.

Another behavior of nature you need to understand about men is that they are **selfish.** They look after their own desires, needs and interests. This behavior is a first cousin to *competitiveness.* Like its first cousin, *selfishness* strives to get its own. It looks out for itself first, and then you. That type of behavior creates a problem, because relationships need to be 50/50. That would mean that half of the time, it's about you, and the other half of the time, it's about him. It could also be viewed as this time it's about you, and the next time is about him. The problem with *selfishness* is that it's always or almost always about the selfish person.

Being *controlling* is another one of the man's behaviors of nature. A man feels the need (by nature) to be in control, to exercise power and authority over the woman and anything that concerns her. This can include family, friends and sometimes even the clothes you wear.

The next couple of behaviors of nature to be aware of are called *arts of the craft*. The arts of the craft are skilled techniques and trickery exercised in producing visual representation while deceiving someone. They are the foundation, or umbrella, that supports and covers all of the aforementioned behaviors of nature. The first is *deception.* Deception is the practice of deliberately making someone believe something other than the truth. Imagine that you met a guy, and before you got involved, you asked him if he was married. He said no. Not only did he say no, he also convinced you that he wasn't by spending a convincing amount of time with you, and perhaps even taking you to his residence or alleged residence. He was able to successfully live this lie long enough to get you in a relationship.

The other art of the craft is *manipulation.* We are all familiar with this concept. It's to control or influence someone in an ingenious or devious way to get them to be an ill-informed, willing participant in a mischievous ploy. For example, you end up discovering that the man who you have been dating and have fallen in love with is married. After the discovery, he tells you that he and his wife are separated and that there is nothing going on between them. He claims that he was afraid if he had told you in the beginning that he was married, you wouldn't have given him a chance. Since you already love him, he is able to further convince you with other eloquent explanations and sincere displays of his affection (not love) about why the only reason he is still living with her until the divorce (which he technically has not applied for) is final, is so he can make it a cordial divorce and not have to lose or pay her as much. He also assures you that they are not sleeping together. So you stay in it, only to find out later (weeks, months, years) that it was all a lie. So manipulation is getting you to stay in the lie that deception got you into in the first place.

Since everything about the man concerning you is directly or indirectly about sex, the indirect things can have more of a problematic effect than you realize. They are the discoveries that you always find out later, and realize that they were right there in your face the whole time. These are a few of the more pertinent behaviors of which you really should be informed and prepared to counteract. These behaviors are used to his advantage and your disadvantage. First of all, all of these are a play on your emotions. It is advantageous for him because his affection that is driven by his lust and motivated by his desire for sex will seem to be everything you are looking for in a relationship. The thoughtfulness, kindness, genuine desire to be with you; these displays of what seem to be favorable and acceptable exhibitions of emotions and behaviors, open your heart and cause you to let him in and accept his advances or offers for a relationship. His advantages are that he knows what his intentions really are, which are rarely what he leads you to believe. Your disadvantage is being a realist. You want to believe in him and what he says because that's your nature. Because you are honest, you easily believe that he is as well. An example scenario would be if someone is cheating, but claims to be faithful, and yet this person is always accusing the other party of cheating due to his or her own infidelity. So, the disadvantage of the woman is because she knows that she is being what she says she is; therefore, she believes he is being what he says he is.

However, it must be reiterated that the nature of the man and the woman are different, almost entirely contrary to each other. Hers tends to be more inward in origin, and his more outward. The most they have in common is the visible and physical components of which God made their bodies. He gave each of them a communication system that consists of an endocrine system and a nervous system. He hardwired them in the same fashion, but gave them different software. (He's mechanically inclined; she's emotionally entwined). However, it's the nervous system that describes them best. It is comprised of two divisions, the central nervous systems, and the peripheral nervous system. The system which best represents her is the central (center) nervous system. The system that best represents him is the peripheral (outer) nervous system. The central nervous system consists of the brain and spinal cord. The brain is the processing center for life's functions, concerns and decisions. The spinal cord receives information, and then sends out instructions. It also connects the central nervous system to the peripheral nervous system.

The peripheral (outer/edge) nervous system, in short, are the muscles that perform and protect. The peripheral consists of four parts: the somatic, autonomic, sympathetic and parasympathetic. One part is designed to receive instructions and carry them out. One part is designed to self-regulate or control everything. The remaining two parts work in concert to protect and to preserve.

Now what we have here is system designs. We did not design them nor can we redesign them, so they are going to do what they are designed to do, be what they are designed to be, and function as they are designed to function.

Be aware of key terms as I describe the peripheral nervous system, which I compare to the man. The peripheral (outer) nervous system regulates or controls all of the body functions whether we are asleep or awake. Additionally, it is responsible for our survival and protection. It is not a sensitive system; it does what it needs to do to survive. The central (inner) nervous system, which I compare to the woman, is responsible for everything overall. It is the brain behind the operation. It works in conjunction with the peripheral nervous system to get the body to do what it needs to do for its betterment as well as for survival. So the two systems, although different, must work in concert to successfully survive. The man, much like the peripheral nervous system, is driven to be in control. The woman, like the central nervous system or information center, needs to be informed, make the decision not to be deceived or manipulated, and make the mental choice to control her situations.

Bear in mind that he is self-centered, selfish and possessive by nature. He has a need to dominate. He is also insensitive by nature. He is more connected to materials than essentials. He has a very strong attraction to the woman. His attraction, however, is very physical, and it is insatiable. He is a hunter or a predator by nature, and his most sought after prey is his female counterpart.

I gave a reference earlier from one of Shakespeare's quotes, "Some are born great, some become great, and some have greatness thrust upon them." The operative words here are "born with", "become," or "thrust into." While women are born with the nurturing essentials for relationships, men round off the other two; they have to become, and they will thrust themselves into a relationship for the sake of sex.

If I had to describe the man in only one word, it would be "sex." The average man's mind is focused on sex eighty-five percent of the time. His need and desires for it are insatiable. Around about the age of fifteen, sex becomes his main drive, and the female becomes the object of his desire. Thus, he enters into an unrelenting pursuit of sexual relations with her, but not just her, he wants every one of them that he can conquer. By his nature, he lacks longevity in monogamy. Though he may start out raw, he quickly evolves into a cunning and conniving hunter who will pursue sex by any means and to any extremes. His over-determined desire for sex is not so much the problem, considering the fact that women also want sex. However, please remember that he is pretty much opposite of you. You could want the same thing but for very different reasons. A woman is much more complex than a man. She has different needs that are independent of one another. She has a physical desire to be intimate, an emotional desire to be loved, and an internal intellectual desire to communicate. She wants a man to meet these needs. But, the man on the other hand, has one basic dominating need or drive, and it's for physical companionship. As the saying goes, "A woman seeks one man to meet her every need, but a man seeks every woman to meet his one need."

There is a saying that goes like this: "If you're going to err, err on the side of caution." So if you are going to err in your judgment of a man, err with the assumption that he is really only after you for sex, rather than thinking he just likes you for you. Women often find this offensive, but know that this is not about what you really are; this is about what he wants you for. So if you proceeded into this thinking the way he thinks, you will be ahead of the game, saving yourself a great deal of heartache and headache. That way, you can protect yourself and your emotions, and ensure that he gets to know you and your character before he gets what he wants. Once he gets what he wants, it's hard for you to get what you want, even if it's for him to know and respect you for you. The fact of the matter is, I'm just telling you the truth, and even if I did not reveal it, it's still the truth.

Men are just being what they are, sexually-driven. Even in the bible, some men had numerous wives. Why? It was due to their insatiable desires for sex, and their lack of temperance to be monogamous. So to fulfill their insatiable desires, and try to seem right while doing it, they married multiple women. King Solomon even had one thousand women. So in conclusion, the aim of this chapter is to leave you with the information necessary for you to protect yourself. Know what you are dealing with when it concerns men. Men don't understand women, and women don't understand men, but it seems that it's the women who always end up getting hurt. This particular chapter is a tool to help you know and understand the man, what drives him and what he is actually thinking, regardless of what he is saying. There is a lot of hope and room for him to change. Some men change by their own doing, but it's usually after they have already hurt many women. Prevent yourself from being a statistic by being informed.

3. Not knowing who you are

The third mistake women make is, not knowing who they are. It would baffle you to see how many women I meet and ask that question only to find that they are unable to give me a conclusive answer. Most would assume that everyone would know who they are because, you are you. But that is not the case. You do not automatically know yourself just because you are you. And not knowing who you are is another one of the main reasons for women ending up in failed relationships.

Getting to know who you are is a lot like getting to know what you like to eat or knowing your appetite. You actually learn this over a period of time, by recalling which foods were pleasing to you and which foods were not. Some things you just couldn't stomach, because you just did not prefer the taste, others were definitely not because you discovered that you were allergic to them. Although you may continue to try foods you are not sure you will enjoy, you do it with caution and ask questions to make sure it does not include the ingredients that you cannot tolerate.

Now in all fairness, women may not consider it necessary to ask themselves who they are, simply because of the many things that they have to be. Besides being mothers to their children, in most cases they also must be fathers, doctors, teachers, motivational speakers, etc. To their husbands they have to be maids, cooks, madams, role players, support systems and therapists. Even to other women they have to be friends and confidants. This is just naming a few roles that women must fill. The few things they do get to know about themselves is how they look, the kinds of clothes they like, the kinds of foods they like, and the places they like to go. Yet, many women do not feel that they get to know who they are because of all the aforementioned roles that do not allow them the time to do so.

By not knowing who you are, you are cheating yourself by forfeiting opportunities to better yourself and your quality of life. The reason most women do not know themselves is because they do not know *how* to get to know themselves. To get know yourself, you must set aside purposely-constructed, soul-searching time. You need quiet time to relax, clear your mind, think, reflect, and have a heart-to-heart with yourself.

The second problem is that if you do not know who you are, then you certainly don't know the kind person who is right for you. Therefore, the likelihood of you becoming involved with someone who you are not compatible with is increased. For that reason, knowing and understanding who and what you are makes you 100% more certain of what you need in a man, which will greatly increase your probability of finding the right man and not another invested failed relationship. So, let's find out who you are.

Who you are is mainly determined by your personality. A person's personality is their unique and relatively consistent pattern of thinking, feelings, acting and behaving. A person's feeling is a result of their thinking. Their actions are a result of their feelings. Their behavior is a result of their actions. Also, remember that the key word given in the previously given description of personality is "consistent." This is due to the fact that an individual's personality is not truly determined merely by isolated conversation, feelings or behavior, but more so by the person's consistent thoughts (conversation), feelings or behavior. So because the term "consistent" refers to repetition with minimal variations, this would suggest that these elements of one's personality would have to be observed over a period of time. You must stop (take your time), look, listen, and observe your person of interest.

Now, let's begin to get to know ourselves. First, we will examine some areas of importance that are vital to you getting to know yourself. The goal is to ascertain or retrieve definitive and conclusive answers about yourself that will later be utilized to put together a personality profile that you will use to qualify a person of interest for you or for the purpose of establishing relationship. You may modify this process to your needs or desires by injecting other questions. And remember, this is all about you, to help you in finding that right connection, so it is imperative that you remain brutally honest. Even if the answers are not favorable for you, we will fix that in the Redefine and Recreate chapter. We will now create a self-evaluation form using an alphabetical format.

We will begin with attitude. What is your *attitude*? First, we should discuss what this means. What is an attitude? It is a complex mental state involving beliefs, feelings, values, dispositions and acting in certain ways at certain times. Your attitude is your personal view, opinion or general feeling about something. It can be mild or loud, reserved or forward. So what is yours? Do you always have to have the last word or do you rarely have anything to say? Do you always think you are right? Are you easily angered, do you fuss a lot, and are you confrontational? Next is b*eliefs*. Your belief system is not genetic; it is usually something that you are taught through real or vicarious experiences. What are your religious and denominational beliefs? Do you believe a woman should work? Do you believe a woman should do all the housework, and the man should handle the outside work? Do you believe a woman should cook every day? If not, how often? *Communication*. Are you a social butterfly? Are you an intellectual conversationalist? Do you like discussing matters of life and family? Do you try to stay abreast of current events? Do you need a man who likes to talk, or do you prefer a man who listens well? *Emotions*. Are you sensitive? Are you dramatic? Are you easily overwhelmed? Are you needy? What about *finances*? Are you a person who believes in a budget and staying out of debt, or do you have a spending problem? Are you *Goal-oriented*? Do you strive to achieve the next level of life? *Interests: (make a list of* things you enjoy doing, and things you want to do. *Love.* Do you fall hard and fast? Do you fall in love easily? Are you in love after the first sexual experience in a new relation-ship? *Optimism.* Do you see the glass as half-full, or half-empty? *Materialism.* Do you like nice things? Do you feel you have to own nice things? How important is the big nice house, the high-end car, the nice jewel-ry? *Personality.* Are you friendly? Do you enjoy laugh-ing, making people laugh, or are you generally a serious person? Are you a people person? Do you like being around lots of friends and family members? Are you a loner? *Recreation.* Do you like to party? Do you drink? Do you smoke? Do you do casual drugs? Do you like to eat out at restaurants often? Do you prefer upscale, average or inexpensive restaurants? Are you very outgoing? *Sex.* Are you very sexual? Do you prefer a lot of sex, very little sex or a moderate amount of sexual relations? Do you need a lot of romancing? You get the picture. This list is not absolute. Continue your list and modify it as it fits your needs. This was just an example.

Now, let's look a bit further into the world of personality. There are two sides to who you are; there is the *true you* and there is the *new you*. Or the *I* and the *me*. The *I* or *true you* is who you are from birth; your character, personality and genetic traits. The *new you*, or the *me*, as it is otherwise referred to, is who you became and are now. This transition usually occurs due to some type of overwhelming circumstances. These circumstances or situations are usually challenging, stressful and more than you can handle or continue to endure without making some type of adjustments. These adjustments may be positive or they may be negative, but they are usually an effort to protect yourself. Each adjustment or change depends on the person and the particular situation. Your character or personality changes usually result from experiences with other people. Perhaps you were repeatedly harassed, picked on, discriminated against or overlooked on job promotions. The list goes on and on. Sometimes you go through these changes due to relationship drama. Maybe you were a victim of domestic abuse and you started fighting back. Maybe you were a repeated victim of infidelity, and you lost trust and grew to be jealous and insecure. Or perhaps you were a victim of verbal abuse or constant verbal conflict and in response, have developed a verbally aggressive personality. So in other words, you may have once been a nice, shy, polite, friendly and giving person. But now you are forward, outspoken, confrontational, aggressive and occasionally even considered to be rude. These behaviors are actually normal; they are psychological defense mechanisms designed to protect you from whatever form of abuse you have been exposed to previously. The problem with these defense mechanisms is that they can affect you in a negative or counter-productive way. But that is not who you are; it is just who you have become. So, part of the goal here is get you back to who you really are and then make you better.

In order to do this, you must accept yourself, for not only what you are, but also for whom you are. This is called the validation. Validating is merely confirming the truth, making a profound connection with ourselves and who we may have become, and can be used to affirm the need for change.

4. Failing to redefine you and recreate yourself

Relationships can be life-changing experiences. They can literally change who you are, taking you from where you were to a place you never thought you would be in life. Some things that you said you would never do, you have done. Some things you thought you would never become, you became. Some things you never thought you would say, you have said. They have the potential to leave you feeling bitter, used, confused, abandoned, rejected and even lost.

The evaluation process that we have just completed helps you to know who you are and where you stand on these issues. It is comparable to taking a trip; you can't get to where you want be without leaving where you are. Therefore, to know your point of origin is equally as important as knowing your destination; that is precisely how the cost of the trip is determined. Yes, relationships can be devastating, life-altering experiences. Yet, even after enduring these unpleasant experiences and changes, most women still find themselves back in them again and again. Sometimes, these retried relationships work, but more often than not, they don't. They could possibly end worse than the previous attempts. In some cases, these failed relationships can have profound short-term psychological effects on a woman's mind, emotions and behavior. These results range from low self-esteem to depression. While in other cases, the psychological effects can be more long-term and extreme, requiring quite a bit of effort to reverse these newly created emotional conditions. This brings us to our fourth, and possibly most pivotal, mistake of all, failure to redefine and recreate. This is necessary for a couple of reasons: (1) Self-recovery, and (2) Preparation for a productive future relationship.

Why is it necessary to redefine and recreate yourself? The truth of the matter is that sometimes you experience sustained emotional duress from dramatic relationships, altering your thoughts, emotions, and behavior, and inadvertently affecting your present or future relationships. This is an example of when good things go bad. Women who were once sound with solid personal and relationship attributes, now have various sorts of emotional baggage, which are all defensive emotional protectors.

This is what happens; your body has a built-in protection system, also known as a psychological defense system. Its primary directive is survival. It survives by adapting, protecting and/or fleeing. Without the proper understanding of this system, it can represent the parent or good friend who tries to help you but ends up hurting you by encouraging you to stay in an unhealthy situation or influencing you to prematurely abandon it.

This built-in protection or defense system acts like an independent internal mind whose sole purpose is your survival. When unexpected dangers or threats occur, the body goes into a fight-or-flight mode to preserve itself. However, if it becomes familiar with the dangers or threats, it will adapt by activating the defense mechanism called coping. Coping is a part of our survival system which attempts to enable the body to adjust itself to its current circumstances in order to survive. This defense mechanism, a standard hardwiring in all of our nervous systems, serves the purpose in helping us deal with the vicissitudes of life. However, when the circumstances are abusive, such as mental abuse, physical abuse or emotional abuse, the psychological adjustment can vary and become harmful instead of helpful, by adapting and preventing you from being able to move forward. Your system does not know the reality of your situation, whether you are in a bad relationship or living in a third world country where living conditions are deplorable, or in a gang-infested city where you have to fight everyday to survive. So it helps you to do what you need to do to survive. If you do not leave (flee), it assumes that you have to stay, so it will help you cope or adjust.

That is why it is important to employ this chapter, "Redefine and Recreate." This process works somewhat similarly to your thermostat. Envision that it is wintertime outside, and it's also uncomfortably cold inside your home. You look at your thermostat, and the thermometer indicates that the temperature is 55 degrees. Well, of course you do not want it to remain at 55 degrees, so what do you have to do? You have to push the thermostat up to 75 degrees or whatever degree you desire. Now, of course, once you do this, your environment is going to change, thus reaching a temperature where you are comfortable. Now, there were five things that had to take place in order for that change to take place. First, you had to realize that you were not comfortable with the current temperature. Secondly, you made a decision to change the temperature. Thirdly, you concluded what it would take to make you comfortable. Fourth, you took the necessary action by actually adjusting the thermometer to a predetermined setting. Lastly, you went on doing what you had to do confidently and expectantly knowing that your environment will soon be what you desired it to be.

We will also implement three other steps needed to complete your redefining and recreating transition. To complete the transition, you will also need to retreat, repair and restart. So let's analyze the five-step process necessary to get your life from where it is to where you want it to be.

Retreat: (to withdraw, go backwards, and escape something hazardous, hurtful or unpleasant; to be alone.) Failed relationships hurt. When you have decided that the relationship is over, you then must retreat. Withdraw from all endeavors of relationships.

Make up in your mind that for now, you are not going to engage in any relationships, relationship discussion or relationship activities. Even dinner or movie dates that are offered with no strings attached. No matter how interestingly unique and different the next guy may seem to be, remember that the situation can turn out the same way the others did so as for now, do not engage.

Repair: (to restore by replacing a part or putting together what is torn or broken). Relationships require so much giving of oneself. Now that you are in remission, it is time to repair. Relationships also can leave you emotionally wounded, and physically and mentally abused. This is the time for you to lick your wounds; this is the opportune time for you to heal. First, engage in activities that will help you relax and free your mind. Treat yourself to a spa day and a nice take-out dinner at home while you watch your favorite show or movie. Go out and buy yourself something nice. Take about a week to focus on relaxation. Then, begin to look back at all that has happened to you and meditate on it. Look at how it started so well and when it started to go wrong. Finally, examine what went wrong. Was it something you did or said? Was it something you allowed or accepted? Look at the first relationship and the ones that followed. Did the same thing happen? As you recount the event, accept the facts, not the blame. Take this time and heal. Men will do what you allow them to do, and they will exploit your weaknesses. So you need to find and repair the breaches.

Redefine: (give a new or different definition to.) Now, it's time to rebuild. We have looked back over your life and relationships and discovered the areas in your life that needed change and repaired them. Now it is time to improve. A relationship can take you into a whole new dimension of life. You first experience elation, then later all the other actions, such as aggravation, frustration, suffocation, complication and eventually, liberation. Through the courses of these failed relationships, you discovered emotional reactions and behaviors that you would have otherwise never displayed, such as angry fits, rages, physical aggressions and verbal abuse. I have known and counseled women who have literally changed because of their emotional duress in relationships. Some started drinking, others started cursing, some took up fighting, some began cheating; the list is endless. These actions or reactions can or have created a new persona in you.

They have changed you, and unless you change the change, this new persona will define you, whereas right now we can say it merely describes what you are now. To redefine is to give a new or different definition. For example, you may be easily angered. You would redefine yourself as calm and drama-free. You may have begun a habit of drinking alcoholic beverages; you would redefine yourself as alcohol-free. You may have subjected yourself to physical abuse; you would redefine yourself as zero-tolerant to physical abuse. You may have subjected yourself to verbal abuse; you would redefine yourself as zero tolerant to verbal abuse.

Recreate (give new life to): Now that we have redefined, let's recreate. It's like a new car or house. First you define (describe) it; that's your blueprint, and then you build it. The prefix re- means to do again. We usually redo something when we have messed it up, destroyed it, lost it, or failed at it. To recreate something is to remake it, which means we must start from scratch. We have to work at it and work at it, build on it and build on it, until it is done. So that is what we have to do. As we have redefined ourselves, now let's recreate ourselves by rebuilding ourselves. Let's take a look at the process. First, look at everything about you, the good and the bad, using the list you made in the previous chapter. Then, employ a few of the "keys to success." (1) Eliminate the bad, and perfect the good. (2)Always think positive and be positive. (3) Build on what you can do, not what you can't. (4) Remember, the one thing you can do (it may not be easy), is change yourself. (5) Remember, the one thing you cannot do is change someone else (but your change, your words and your ways may influence this person to make the decision to change.)

So, we take the list we made and divide it into two parts, a positive and a negative. Then read through it and list your values, which are the good moral things that are important to you, such as spending quality family time, communicating or going to church. Increasing your value is similar to getting out of debt, and usually the reason one desires to get out of debt is because of financial woes. Increasing one's income is not always an option, so instead, you decrease your outgoing (stop spending), which consequently is the first step of saving. So what we are doing here is turning our negativity into positivity. Essentially, this is the purpose of the lists, to turn the negative into the positive, or in other words, eliminate the negative. There are two principal ways of achieving that. One is converting and the other is eradicating. Here is an example of converting. Pretend for a moment that your negative behavior is jealousy. Jealousy is usually derived from an insecurity, which creates a need to control. To eliminate this behavior, it is necessary to rid yourself of the insecurity. This can be done with a three-step process: (1) Confession, (2) Contentment and (3) Commitment. Confession is good for the soul. Contentment is accepting your insecurities and making them your strengths instead of your weaknesses. And commitment involves committing to be the best that you can be, especially in the area of insecurity. This converts your insecurity into security, your need to control into freedom, and your jealousy into trust. The idea of converting is to change something from one thing to another.

Now, let's look at an example of eradicating. Imagine that you had a problem with alcohol. You admit that you have a problem with it (confession is good for the soul) then take the necessary steps to quit. Now in this case, you did not change drinking into something else; you got rid of it, stopping it altogether. That is eradicating, which means to get rid of something completely.

So, the next step is to eliminate our negatives. Once we have accomplished that, then we advance to our positive values that we previously listed and begin connecting with them. To achieve this, we take each value one at a time, profess it and connect it, which essentially is to apply it. Here we see how well each of the values that we chose actually fit our lives. Sometimes we will realize that a particular value fails to work to its full capacity. This usually indicates a need to make internal acclimation adjustments. In such cases, we determine which steps are required to achieve our values, and then we begin to execute them. One way to accomplish this is to write the value down on a piece of paper that can be kept in your pocket for easy access. In addition, write what you need to do to complete this value and read it up to five times a day. Repeat this with as many values as necessary. If the values you have listed are lengthy, then read them each time verbatim until you have successfully memorized them.

Restart: *(take up or begin new)*. To restart is to begin new. To be quite honest, you will most likely involve yourself in another relationship, even though you might feel like you never want to again; it is simply human nature to be in relationships. You should be thoroughly prepared after applying everything you have learned in this book. When you restart, do not resort to making any compromises. More importantly, do not give in to sex before you are married, and do not marry before you really get to know him. Apply what you have learned from this book. Remember, to restart is to begin new; that means it's a new you, so don't make old mistakes. Repair yourself, redefine yourself and recreate yourself.

To summarize, we have discussed four topics as part of the restoration process: (1) what you are, which helps you to understand why you love and connect the way you do, (2) what he is which assists you in understanding why he loves the way he does, or *doesn't*, (3) and who you are, which is understanding your values, which for many, can be a first-time experience, (4) and then redefine and recreate. This will help make you the best you that you can be. The next step is to increase your value.

5. Failing to increase
your values

The fifth mistake women make is not increasing their values. When dealing with men, it is important for women to know and increase their values. Men come expecting, not respecting. Men will make changes, even though most changes are temporary, and their level of respect for you can increase, but only to the level you require. This has to be attained through actions that supersede your words. A man cannot do any more than you let him, so it is crucial that you think about your long-term needs rather than your short-term desires.

Let's first gain an understanding of the word "value," by analyzing two of the most appropriately applicable dictionary definitions. The first is *"the accepted principles or standards of a person"* and the other is *"to rate someone according to their perceived worth."* These are powerful and empowering statements. They are powerful because they allow you to say who you are, and empowering because they allow you to be who you say you are. Now, let's examine both of those in greater detail.

"The accepted principle or standards of a person" [the breakdown.] A principle is your ethical standard. The concept of standard refers to the level of quality accepted as normal and to be ethical means to be consistent with agreed principles of correct moral conduct. Last, but not least, to be moral means behaving decently and honorably. So the moral is, do not do in the beginning what you are supposed to do in the end (have sex.) A person has to accept whatever principles or standards you set, not what you say. So it is important that you reexamine the mistakes or indiscretions you have committed in your past and implement the necessary changes.

The second definition was *"to rate someone according to their perceived worth."* The word "perceive," means three things: (1) *To notice*, which is to observe or study in a particular way, (2) *To understand*, which is to come to know someone by learning or hearing (3) and *to comprehend,* which is to include something as part of a larger whole. To notice, understand and comprehend, are to the word perceive, as fingers, thumb and palm are to the word hand. Either one missing word or part reduces or limits its maximum intended use or capability. Whether you realize it or not, a man may not know the tri-part meaning of the word "perceive," but his mind will certainly process the aspects of it. You may not have known the tri-part meaning of the term either, but you certainly will send them. This is the large part of the problem; women send the wrong message, that the end is conclusive of the means. Well, that is precisely what we are going to fix.

Your value is what someone accepts it to be, but that person cannot accept anything less than what you give. Therefore, if a man wants to be with you, he has to accept you for who you are. He has to accept the rules or standards that you have set, or you do not have to be with him. You should not feel any obligation nor should you feel a need to give in to any of his pressures or demands for fear that you will lose a good, successful or attractive man. The only thing you will lose by giving in to him prematurely is your self-worth and self-respect. By giving in to him, you have just given him the power to set your standards. The result is that he will want you to do what he wants you to do, whenever he wants you to do it. Additionally, his level of respect for you will dwindle significantly, sometimes resulting in verbal and/or physical abuse. He will only abuse you because he has either accessed you, or simply because he has tested it and discovered that he can. A man will treat you either how he can or how he has to. How he "can" is *his* standard; how he "has to" is *your* standard. Do not let his standards become your standards. You do not have to, and neither should you, accept any mistreatment; you have the power to determine how you will be treated. As stated earlier, many women are not aware of how to set or establish their values. Valuing yourself is the first phase of respect from others, especially men, and it is the direct path to you receiving the treatment that you deserve.

Part of the problem is that you know what you want from the relationship, he knows what he wants, and in most cases, those are two different things. When a man is interested in you and becomes involved with you, for the most part, you will only be as valuable to him as he perceives your worth of yourself to be. So just because he expresses a lot of interest in you and seems to be willing to do almost anything for you does not necessarily mean that he actually values or respect you. He does what he does because of what he wants. This is not about you; it's about him. It's about his affection and his lust; that is simply what men do. So, do not allow his admirable actions be mistaken as him actually being an admirable man. Your values do determine how far a man will go for you, but not what he will do for you; his lust determines that. Men all have one common dominating drive, and it is sex. You need to understand that to every man, every woman starts out as a sex object. Although he may have a profound interest in a particular woman, it usually all revolves around sex. Your desire to hold out and be respected presents a challenge, a test and a quest for him. His nature is predesigned and determined to accept and conquer. It is not at all uncommon that he just views you as a desirable physical attraction, because he has not yet perceived your value or worth, and he really does not initially care about that. He will, however, have an opinion of you. He will also have an intention, a strategy and a goal to conquer you. His intention is to sleep with you as soon as he can. His strategy is to do whatever it takes to achieve this. Some of it he makes up as he goes, but he does have pre-plans, which are things that he knows women either, like, love or adore. These are things such as dinners, movies, money, flowers, jewelry, etc. His goal is to spend a certain amount of money and time within his predetermined level of commitment and determination. The point when you give in to him sexually may be the point that he rates you. This set value of yourself ultimately determines his perceived worth of you and rate of you.

So how do you establish your perceived worth? This is done by putting first things first. Remember, you know who you are, and what your values are, but he doesn't know and he doesn't really care. Although you may say what you are about, and he hears you, he will still attempt to conquer you. Regardless of your spoken values, they really are set and determined by your actions. Remember, your perceived worth is what is *noticed, understood, and comprehended,* or in other words, it is what he sees, what he hears, and what he has come to know.

Let's take a look at the first aspect of the three parts of being *noticed.* This is the visual part of the process.

This is when he first sees you and decides that he wants you. At this point, his attraction is lust. There is absolutely nothing you can do about this; that's just his nature as a man. He continues to try to get a read on you; he is looking for accessibility (to get you to smile or hold a free and willing conversation.) He equates this as your acceptance of him. He pays attention to how you dress, your body language, and observes your responses, reactions and replies to his conversation, his questions and his actions. So carry yourself in a proper way. Refrain from being flirtatious, from touching him, from purposely doing or saying anything to draw any attention to your body. Do not engage in inappropriate conversations on subjects such as sex or condoning cheating. If you want him to respect you, then you must first respect yourself. Carry yourself appropriately whether day or night; he is taking mental notes on everything. You do not have to give it up to let him know you care (no matter how badly you may want to.) A man's values depend on him, and they vary from one man to the next even though most men do share the nature described in "What He Is."

So even though you may do a great job representing your values, the man still may not want to make the ultimate commitment. What do you do? Write him off. Do not continue investing your time waiting for him to stop playing and get serious. Move on; other men will always come seeking. Just apply the things you have learned, and it will work out. The second part is to *understand.* To understand someone, you must listen and learn. This part takes time. It's not about just saying it, it's about giving what you say time to settle and be proven. This part is not about telling him what you like to do as entertainment or recreation. It is more about your values as a person, and these are not things that he can easily manipulate. Even though you tell him your values, he is still trying to size you up and see what he can do to get you to do what he wants, which is to be sexual. Then it's the *comprehending,* the last part of the process. Here he is trying to see if your actions are consistent or contrary to what he has observed and heard. It is pertinent that you do and be what you have professed. No matter how badly you want to make temporary exceptions, do not compromise or improvise. It is important that you use this time to properly establish the kind of relationship that you want from a man. No matter what he came thinking you would do, no matter what kind of confidence he has in himself of being able to get women to do what he wants them to do, you can change, determine and set his value of you, by the values that you have set, sustained and consistently maintained on display before him. However, you must be sincere and committed to yourself to do and be what you say.

6. *Failing to increase your worth*

T he sixth mistake women make is not increasing their worth. Worth is fundamental. No matter where you may be in your life right now, single, married, widowed, divorced, mother or have no children, you need to consider your worth (external value) and increase it. So many women take on the roles of dedicated housewives, dedicated working wives and mothers, or dedicated working single mothers, so committed to their roles, responsibilities, and obligations that they seem to forget about themselves. To increase your worth is to be all that you were purposed and designed to be. To do this, it is necessary for you to take the time to discover you, your capabilities, desires, gifts and talents. Then you need to make provisions to pursue them. The two entities that keep you from doing that are children and men. You're either raising the children or probably raising your man. Well, you can do both, and still take care of you too. Remember, one of a woman's many strengths is the ability to multi-task.

You must also keep in mind that your children are only going to be with you for a limited time. From my many years of coaching and counseling, I have found that some of the men are only going to be there for a limited time also. So many women feel that they need to at least wait until their children are graduated from high school before they explore relationships. Well as a coach, it is not my role to make decisions for you; I only advise or recommend. So, if you feel that you need to wait, then you should wait. But there are two things that happen while you are waiting. One is that you lose certain windows of opportunities, and the other is that the desire to take on such a challenge greatly decreases after a certain age. There are also two things that happen when you decide to improve your worth while the children are still children. One is that as you start to improve yourself by pursuing your gift or talent, you improve you self-confidence and self-esteem, as well as your self-worth. The other thing is as you start to improve, your desire for your children's success also increases. Naturally, you already want them to be greater than you are anyway, so when you become more, your standards and expectations for your children just increase a whole lot more. So by improving your worth, everyone connected to you improves their worth. Your question may be, *if I have kids, how and when do I start?* You first need to identify the pertinent time set aside for your children, and the times when you are free. Determine a consistent schedule and plan your time around that. Due to the highly technological world we live in today, there are plenty of ways and opportunities via the internet to attain what you need and desire in the way of education and training.

If you are single and without children, this is really the time for you to aggressively seek to improve your worth. There are two reasons why. The first is the fact that not having children allows you a mountain of time that would otherwise be obligated time. This allows you to pursue and attain you goals, gifts and talents in a much shorter time frame, which is quite important. The second reason is that if you are single, you avoid an external opponent, which typically is your man. As stated earlier, men are controlling, and competitive. Your attending school to better yourself translates to him as you being better than him, thus being less dependent on him. Although they rarely admit it, this poses a problem for most men. They may start to complain that you are not spending enough time with them. They may ask why you feel you need to attend school when it's taking away your time to do things together. These men have endless lines of Rationale to sway you away from school. But this is your time to shine.

As women, I challenge you to answer the call, even as I challenged the men. Men need to take a stand and be the fathers of the world, accepting their responsibilities, and imparting the internal insights and provisions that God gave them to teach their children how to survive, achieve and succeed in this world (see my book, *The Man in Me*.)

As women, you are the mothers of this world. Every man, woman, boy or girl came from you. When you look at what you are now, compared to what you were after your first relationship, you would undoubtedly agree that you have grown significantly. Who you are and what you stand for represent what they are and what others will be. The more you are, the more they will be. Do not be like the many women I talk to who are not what they feel they could have or should have become, who wished their parents would have encouraged or pushed them harder to accomplish more in their lives. Do not perpetuate the cycle. So start now, discover your gift, talent or passion, and pursue it. If you have no idea what your passion is, then think about what you have always wanted to do. Ponder on something right now that you enjoy doing. Then look into ways that you can pursue it, do it and become it.

Sometimes what you are called to do may be a bit outside of your comfort zone. You may have exceptional insight on much needed subject matters, but do not desire to speak publicly to audiences. Yet, you feel that this is what you are to do. In this case, you must pursue it, do it and become it. Your passion may be in politics, real estate, the medical field, agriculture, animals, social science, culinary arts, business, teaching, counseling or other various areas of expertise. If it is something that would require you to enroll in school, think about it, calculate the cost, make your plans and do it.

7. Failing to protect your worth

The seventh mistake often made by women is not protecting their worth. Protecting your worth is really about you; it is about not losing your identity. At this point, you have already increased your worth. You have done what you needed to do. You have redefined what needed to be redefined. You have repaired what needed to be repaired. And you have recreated yourself to become what you need to be. Now it is time to protect your worth. Protecting your worth is refusing to let someone stifle your growth or steal your drive. Sooner or later, some guy will accost you, and because you want to be accosted, you will find yourself in a relationship. This could be good; **there are problems in relationships, but relationships are not the problem.** Relationships require sacrifices, and a sacrifice requires you to give up something valued. Mistakes women have made in the past include offering themselves to be the sacrifice, putting their careers on hold, and not utilizing that degree, gift or talent that they have worked so hard to attain. Even though there are sacrifices that need to be made, they often can be made in other areas. Most of what needs to be done can be accomplished through a good financial plan. There are many ways that you can increase your income, mainly by revising you outgoing, and eliminating some of the extras. There are many places you can obtain financial planning, just search the web. One thing you do not need to do is compromise your true self. Sometimes men will try to get you to sacrifice you. You may be going to school/college, seeking a degree to pursue a field of passion. He may tell you that you need to let that wait. There are many other ways you can accomplish the same goal without giving up your dream. Be what you were when you met him. If you make any changes, there should be a gain, not a loss. You have worked hard to get where you are; don't give it up. Protect your worth.

8. Failing to properly connect your worth

We have covered seven of the eight mistakes that women make when it concerns relationships, which are not knowing what you are, not knowing what he is, not knowing who you are, not redefining and recreating, not increasing your values, not increasing your worth, and not protecting your worth. The eighth mistake that women often make is not knowing how to connect your worth. It was earlier affirmed that God has given us an innate desire for copulation, which is a euphemism for sex. Why? Because that is how the cycle of life is perpetuated. So there is a great chance that if you are not currently in a relationship, you are going to be involved in one, whether it is for the eighth time or the first time. My role is to help you make this connection be the right connection.

Making the right connection is not about getting involved with someone who is exactly like you. Initially, that would seem to be a positive connection, because you would share the same interests and ideas. But that would also mean that you would also share the same faults. You would probably think that's okay, since you live with yourself and your own faults everyday anyway. But the truth of the matter is, we really do not realize or recognize our own faults as problems, even though we all possess them. We have an uncanny ability to develop immunity to our own faults but not so easily to someone else's.

The chances for a positive connection would be more likely after reading and applying what you have learned from this book, because part of our exercise was identifying faults and eradicating them. Of course that would only work provided that he read the book and made the appropriate changes also. But the chances of you finding that man who likes everything you like and dislikes everything you dislike, would be rare.

It is reasonable to be different in positive ways, however, not in negative ways. Contrast is good; conflict is not. A positive dissimilarity would be like your hands; you have a left hand and a right hand. The left hand has a thumb on the right side of it (looking at them palm side down), but the right hand has the thumb on the left side of it, and the fingers of each hand are placed on opposite sides as well. However, the two hands work together in perfect harmony like they were made for each other. So although they are opposite, they have the same things in common, four fingers and a thumb.

Although they have the same things in common, a pointer finger, a middle finger, a ring finger and a pinky finger, they are two separate entities, often working together, yet rarely ever doing exactly the same things, such as when you text, type, cook, clean, play a piano and so on. So again, contrast is good, but conflict is not.

In most cases, women end up in conflict rather than contrast. When you seek to find your good connection, you either discover it by a plan or by plight. Plight refers to unfortunate circumstances, which is what most women's relationships transpire into, a set of unfortunate circumstances. So, let's look at a plan. God's word says that without a vision, the people perish. A vision is a mental picture or a plan. You may be familiar with the common saying, which I will paraphrase: "People don't plan to fail, they fail to plan." To make the right connection, there must be a plan.

Now the plan we will use is a five-step process. Step one: *Take your time.* Step two: *Take inventory.* Step three: *Take account.* Step four: *Take interest.* Step five: *Take the chance.* All of these steps are extremely important and are all of equal *importance.* This process will not be successful without each step being employed in sequence and executed in its entirely in the manner in which it was intended. Let's discuss the first step.

Step 1: Take your time

Relationships require nurturing and growth, which takes a significant amount of time. Time is truly of the essence, and for a number of reasons. **In time we will grow older, with time we get wiser, and some time we get hurt, but through time we heal.** It is important to take your time. If you are just getting out of a relationship, take your time. Do not jump out the frying pan into the fire; get out of the kitchen. Examine your wounds, take time to heal, retreat, repair, redefine, recreate and then restart. The third chapter of Ecclesiastic also gives us several examples of the uses, and purposes of time.

The reason this five-step process must begin with time is because the other four steps have to be timed in order to be effective. This process will be equivalent to building a four-story building; time is the foundation, taking inventory is the first floor, taking account is the second floor, and so on. How do we employ time? There are only two things you can do with time; use it wisely, or waste it. The only way to use time wisely is to have a plan. If you do not have a plan, you are wasting time, and if you are wasting time, you are wasting life, because life is short.

A plan first begins in your mind. From there, you should write it down. Why do I need a plan? A plan provides structure, strategy, purpose, and a time frame, which creates a schedule that transcends into production, thus making you a productive person instead of someone just wasting time and life.

So, the first step in making a good connection is taking your time. In order to take your time, it means you allocate a predetermined amount of time to methodically invoke the steps we previously discussed. It is critical that you do not rush into a relationship. The amount of time that I recommend to properly treat a relationship before you consummate it is one year. That's one year before engaging in sexual relations, which should be, after marriage. Realistically, that rarely happens anymore considering the highly charged, sexually acclimated society we live in today. But when it is regarding relationships, time is crucial, so you must plan to wait before getting sexually involved; sex changes things. **If he can't wait for your worth, then he's not worth your wait.** Most women that I council concerning failed relationships believe (as they speak from retrospect) that if they had taken more time to know the man, to know back then what they found out later, it would have significantly changed the choices and decisions that they made concerning the men in their lives.

Just as it takes time for wounds to heal, it also takes time for things to be revealed. Women do not completely understand the mind of a man just like a man does not totally understand the internal workings, needs, emotions and desires of a woman. But that is fine; most people don't know a tree by its leaves. But if you give it time, in its season, it will undoubtedly bear fruit. At that point, you will know if it's an orange tree, tangerine tree, etc. and likewise with the man, you just have to give him time to reveal what he is.

Time, however, in and of itself, will not reveal the things you really need to know about a man. Those things are revealed through the remaining four steps. However, they are ineffective without the proper allotment of time. You can wait a whole year before getting physically involved, but if you fail to ask the right questions, address the right issues, do the right things, then the wait will be of no avail. So then that time is wasted without the proper application of the other four steps. Conversely, the other four steps are wasted without the proper application of time.

So we have discussed the importance of time, the benefits of using it, and the perils of not. So, with every step, keep these three key things in mind: Take your time, have a plan, and follow through. So, how should time be used? There should be a specific amount allocated to each step. An example of allocation would be three months to "take inventory," three months to "take account," three months to "take interest," and three months to "take the chance." The reason you need to allocate time to each individual step is to maximize the potential of that step.

Step 2: Take inventory (what's there)

The most common reason for relationship failure is incompatibility, which refers to making the wrong connection or choosing someone who does not possess the qualities that you need for a successful relationship. Notice that I said the qualities *you* need; this is about you, about you knowing you and knowing what you need in relationship. This does not mean he was a bad guy or did not have any good qualities, or that he would not flourish or succeed in another relationship. This is solely referring to whether or not he has what you need. We have allotted three months to this step. Let's see how it works. What is inventory? It is a report of what is alleged to be present at or inside a particular place, space, site, or in this case, a person. Using this definition, we need to take inventory to know him on the inside, to determine if he has what you need. You find this out by asking the right questions. To do this, compare it to a system to which you can already relate. Let's use Wal-Mart, for example. You are going to be the customer or consumer, and He will be the store.

Just like with Wal-Mart, we want him to be our one-stop shop. In order for the store to successfully pass this test, it has to readily and consistently carry what you need, want or desire. The store needs to first know the purpose of being a store, then determine if it has the goods or means to get the goods and consistently maintain the supply in demand. Additionally, there would be specialty items the store needs to obtain also. If the store wants to be your store of choice, it will work hard to meet your demands and exceed your expectations. Now remember, you must take your time, have a plan and follow through. The plan is to communicate with the intent and purpose of finding out if he (the store) has, and is, what you are looking for in a man. The inventory will reveal this if conducted properly.

Inventory is utilized from two perspectives, the consumer and the proprietor. Consumer perspective is primarily concerned with the products a store carries, and chooses its store based on that vendor carrying what is needed or wanted. The proprietor perspective is concerned with everything in the store, not just having what the consumer wants, but also *not* stocking anything that is considered offensive or unacceptable to the consumer. Now thus far, you have been placed in the position of the consumer, to make sure that he has what you need. Now is the time to step into the role of the proprietor, because you are also the owner of very valuable property, *you*. The mistake that most women make from the consumer perspective is that when they see enough of the qualities they like in a man, they choose to accept him as a relationship partner. Then they later discover (the proprietor's perspective) that the man has unacceptable ways or behaviors.

The proprietor has to know what things that store needs in order for it to succeed and exactly which things will cause it to fail. As proprietor of your own self, it is your responsibility to know yourself, to know what you need in your life (business) in order for you to be happy and have a successful relationship. In addition, your role as proprietor also means that it is your duty to block the behavior that is offensive or unacceptable from your relationship (business) as well.

Let's look at the first two steps in getting to know a man, time and questions. Take your time, and ask the right questions. Utilize the list that you created in Chapter 3, "Who you are." Furthermore, reflect on unacceptable acts, behaviors or habits of the man or men from past relationships, and form them into inventory questions. Get to know who he is by knowing *what* he is, and get to know what he is by knowing what is *in* him. A successful inventory system means a successful production system, which ultimately means a successful business. If you use the same system for relationships, you will acquire a successful relationship. Businesses also use the list to determine the level of demand on the items that they have determined a need to stock, and use their space accordingly, providing more space to the items in higher demand.

Relationships work in basically the same fashion. You can use the same formula of supply in demand. Since you know yourself, you know what you need more of, some things you need a lot of, and some things you only need or want a little of. You need to know if your proprietor can meet those demands. So as you can see, it is necessary to use both perspectives; consumer and proprietor. As the consumer, you make the list, and you also make the determination as to which items are of most importance and which will make the most impact. In essence, you decide which items should receive the most space or time. Now this does not mean that the smaller items are not equally as important or do not deserve an equal amount of time in their own right (remember the little foxes spoils the vine.) Everything is important and anyone who has been in a relationship for any amount of time knows that most arguments are about the smaller things, the little silly things that really should not even matter.

It was previously discussed that inventory is the recorded or reported list of items said to be inside the facility. So, you have met him, you like him, and now you are talking to him. You are at the point of inventory, to see what he has in stock, and you are going to use your list that you comprised in Chapter four. Your list will serve as your supply in demand. This is the part where you get to ask the guy the right kinds of questions, to see what kind of store he is, and determine if he will get your business. This step is ensued only if you are interested in the man. So, let's imagine that he accosted you in the department store and began to make small talk. Let's say the two of you conversed about the weather, the oil spill, or the second coming of the Lord; any of these topics are suitable for icebreakers. However, if you are interested in him, he is interested in you, and he expresses this interest, then you need to get on to the elimination or pre-qualification conversation. This step basically entails a few questions such as, *Are you married? Are you involved in a relationship? Are you seeing someone?* Even though these are all basically one question, you must ask it three different ways when communicating with men, because if he is interested in you, he will answer you technically at worst, and lie at best. If the answer to any of those questions is yes, then keep it moving. No exceptions.

So let's he says he is not involved with anyone and you give him your phone number (by the way, I recommend you do your communication by phone and not in person.) When the two of you talk again, you want to get on to the qualifying questions at some point in that conversation. When asking these questions, be subtle, creative and natural with your questions; do not conduct the conversation as if you are conducting an interview. Keep the questions appropriate: What kind of work do you do? Where do you work? Do you own a vehicle? What kind of vehicle do you own? Do you have a driver license? Now the questions so far and the ones yet to come may sound kind of personal or interrogational, but relationship is personal, and that is the direction where this is headed, which means he will get to know you in a very personal way, so you need to know very personal things about him. Some of these little questions, if not asked, can make a big difference later on down the road. If he checks out there, then you move on to the curious questions. Get AIDS tests. Do you believe in abstinence before marriage? Do you believe in women's liberation? What do you believe a woman's role is in a marriage? What is your feeling on a woman making more money than a man? What is your religious preference? Do you have children? Are you active in their lives? How is the relationship between you and their mother? Do you want more kids? Do you pay child support or alimony? Do you do or buy extra for them? Are you abusive? Do you cook, clean or wash clothes? Think of more questions to ask, and ask them. Again, do not make it an interrogation, but do ask questions nonetheless.

At any point when you hear anything that would be considered a red flag, make a written note of it in your *Relationship Red Flag Book*. Yeah, you need to start a "Relationship Red Flag Book." At that time or in the next conversation, further investigate the matter. You need to get an acceptable degree of satisfaction in your *red flag resolutions* section of your book before you allow yourself to take any further interest. You may, however, go on to other areas of conversations to prove them.

In the final part of the inventory, you need to know how both of your personalities line up together. People are either introverted or extroverted. It is not necessary that you have identical personality types, but being different can be a problem. In short, an introverted personality is reserved, quiet and homely. An extroverted personality is outgoing, friendly and dominant.

Introverted -	**extroverted**
(1) reserved, unsociable -	outgoing, sociable.
(2) less intellectual, concrete -	more intellectual, abstract.
(3) affected by feelings -	emotionally stable.
(4) submissive, humble -	dominant, assertive.
(5) serious -	happy go lucky.
(6) expedient -	conscientious.
(7) timid -	venturesome.
(8) tough minded -	sensitive.
(9) trusting -	suspicious.
(10) practical -	imaginative.
(11) forthright -	shrewd, calculating.

(12) self-assured -   apprehensive.

(13) conservative -   experimental.

(14) group-dependent -   self-sufficient.

(15) undisciplined -   controlled.

(16) relaxed -   tensed.

This may all seem like a lot of work, but in the end, it is worth it. There was a hardware store about a mile from where I lived. But they never had all the items I needed to complete a project; I always had to visit another store. Now the other store was about ten miles away, but they always had in stock everything I needed to complete the job. As a bonus, they provided courteous and helpful service. At the store which was closer in proximity to my home, it seemed that the employees headed in the opposite direction as soon as they would see you coming to ask a question. Even though the store with the superior product selection and customer service was inconvenient in location and took longer to reach, the employees had a reputation for consistently going out of their way to help the customer, and I gladly drove the distance for all of my projects.

Step 3: Taking account (what's not)

The third step is taking account. One meaning of the word "account" is to have a particular quality. Another is to do things in a way that does justice to one's ability or character. In other words, this is show time. In step number two, you got acquainted by gathering information or building a profile. Here in this step, you want to see if he is what he says he is. In step two, I recommended that you communicated by phone. Now it is time to amend that, but you must keep your feeling in perspective. Although you have selected him as a prospect, at this point, you must still see him as a pretender, an academy award performer who is playing the role to get the part or parts that he desires. Now this guy may turn out to be the one, and hopefully he will because that is what we want, but in the meantime, we have to take the preliminary precautionary measures to keep you from getting hurt or wasting your time on someone who is not the one.

It is time to see if what you heard from him adds up. So right here, you are not lady love; you are Inspector See-right, because your goal here is to see if he is right for you. So take your time here and remember that this guy may very well be playing a game.

Therefore, you can expect him to be courteous, polite, thoughtful and maybe even sensitive. This is a must for him, because if he does not encompass those things now while he is trying to impress you, then you cannot expect him to do them later in the relationship. So, this is the time to make sure he is what you want in a man and is capable of doing the things you need and want done.

Let's commit three months to this stage. Remember, our first two stages were more idle than action; they consisted more of listening and learning. Our next stage, however, is an action stage, which consists of more actual doing than the previous stages. In the last stage, we created an inventory list. This is the stage where you looked through the stockroom to see if it is there. Here you will take it one step further. You will go out on a few dates, about once a month. The point here is to take it slow, and you want to communicate that message clearly and concisely. If he is really into you, he will wait faithfully. If he doesn't, then let him go. It is also important here that you do not compromise. If you are worth his wait, he will wait. When you go out the first two or three times, do not go to places where you cannot converse, such as a movie theater or locations where the music is loud. Use this time to have casual talk but also conformation time. Ask him again some of the more important questions from your inventory list so that you can see if the answers are consistent and if his reactions and expressions are settling and reassuring.

You also want to see if you are satisfied with his manners, chivalry and behavior, as well as his anxiety and patience between dates. You want him to anxiously want to see you between dates, but not cross any boundaries.

Step 4: Taking interest

This is our fourth stage, and it is an active stage. This is where you take it to the next level. You have selected it, requested it, inspected it, and now you are testing it. This means that you will take him for a real road test, a three-month road test. Your goal is to see his true self. You may feel as if you are asking a lot of this man, but not only should you ask a lot, you should actually expect a lot from him. After all, women not only give a lot, they take a lot. Keep in mind that he is not the only one waiting, and he is not the only one who wants to be intimate, so this is not just about seeing if he thinks you are worth his wait; this is really about seeing if he is worth *your* wait. So in this stage, you will do everything except sexual affection (no kissing, rubbing, grinding, oral, or anything physical), but otherwise behave as though you are in a relationship. Begin to see him often, very often, everyday if you choose. Do the kinds of things you like to do and go to the kinds of places you enjoy. Hang out with the kinds of friends and family you like, and see how he reacts. It is important to watch his reactions. Until the relationship is consummated, you have to watch and listen for the things he does not say more than what he does say because he is smart. He is waiting until he's in, until he has your heart before he starts to say what he wants to say. So listen with your eyes and heart more than with your ears.

Step 5: Take the chance

With over twenty years in the electrical field, the rules existed long before that, and still are now that you must make a good connection. If you don't, the wire will burn down and you will find yourself out of power. It did not matter so much as to the size of the wire. It could be a big wire going to a small wire or a small wire going to a big wire. What really mattered were the connectors. The connector is the component which joins two separate pieces of wires together. It is one component that has two hollow tube-like moldings for the two separate pieces of wires to fit into. Then the three are compressed together and becomes one solid piece. The hollow molds that make up the component come in all different individual sizes to specifically join together the wires that are needed to be joined. The size of the wire does not matter, the connector does. An improper connector means an improper connection, causing the wires to overheat and burn and resulting in a loss of power.

Whether working on power lines, houses or businesses, it has been a proven fact over and over again that the wires had to be brushed down to remove debris or contaminants, greased with an electrical inhibitor, and then fitted with the right connector. Even with everything else done properly, the connection is still no good if the proper amount of torque is not used to secure the connection.

What does this mean in relationship talk? It means that even if you have the right connector, your relationship still needs to be rid of all debris or contaminants, such as old boyfriends or girlfriends, other negative influential relationships or bad habits. Any of these issues can ruin what would otherwise be a good, solid relationship. The connector is that tie or bond, that glue that is going to keep you together. Do not get that confused with the chemistry that put you together. *What gets you together is usually way different than what keeps you together.* Your connector is a compilation of your core values, morals, personalities and traits,

So, the important aspect in making the right connection is having the right connectors, the qualities that tie you to the person. You should be the cornerstone of the relationship; he should edify you, highly esteem you, really respect you and truly adore you. His role is treating you with kindness, thoughtfulness, tender love and care. This should be the case not only in the initial phase, but continually, not only when he is getting what he wants, but most importantly, when he is not.

A good relationship should also be tested and tried. When the relationship is on the rocks, you should still know that he is there for you. You should have assurance that if you needed anything in that very time, he will do it for you, get it for you or give it to you. So, take what you have learned here, practice it and apply it. So now go in patience, and your next relationship shall be your best relationship. God bless you and your relationship.

Note from the Author

I'd like to thank you for reading this book. I really put my heart in it because it's my passion to help others. It's a part of my dream to help make our relationships healthier and longer lasting and I hope this book helps give you some insight as to how you can do that. If there is anything that you are unsure on or if you'd like to dig deeper or work with me one on one to better understand more about yourself, men, and relationships as a whole please feel free to contact me at Asktonygsr@yahoo.com and cc my son at tony@tonygaskins.com just in case I miss the email. One of us will reach out to you and set up your coaching session. It's my hope that this book has helped you answer some questions you may have had. Again, thank you for your support of this mission.

Special Thanks

I want to first thank my Heavenly Father and Jesus Christ our Lord and Savior for originating and orchestrating this book. Also for giving me the strength, wisdom, knowledge, and understand to write it. In life it is our job as parents to protect, provide, lead, guide, coach, challenge, counsel, instruct, and inspire our kids. Well sometimes our kids challenge and inspire us. I would like to give a special thank to my son Tony A. Gaskins Jr. who is a very wise young man, for his inspiration and motivation. I also want to give a special thanks to my daughter Latesha V. Gaskins for giving me feedback on the book She is a very wise young lady. I thank their mother for her commitment, dedication, and sacrifices that she's made for them. Lastly, I'd like to give a special thanks to Vannant Baker for her input and feedback also.

Made in the USA
Lexington, KY
05 March 2014